BOOK OF EASY TUBA SOLOS

Edited by **Charles Daellenbach** of The Canadian Brass

■

All Selections Performed by **Charles Daellenbach** on tuba, and pianist Patrick Hansen

■

Plus Piano Accompaniments Only

CONTENTS

In a generally progressive order of difficulty.

The instrument pictured on the cover is a CB50 Tuba from The Canadian Brass Collection, a line of professional brass instruments marketed by The Canadian Brass.

To access audio visit:
www.halleonard.com/mylibrary

Enter Code
2028-6834-2004-0359

ISBN 978-0-7935-7252-6

HAL•LEONARD®

www.canadianbrass.com
www.halleonard.com

Contact Us:
Hal Leonard
7777 West Bluemound Road
Milwaukee, WI 53213
Email: info@halleonard.com

In Europe contact:
Hal Leonard Europe Limited
42 Wigmore Street
Marylebone, London, W1U 2RN
Email: info@halleonardeurope.com

In Australia contact:
Hal Leonard Australia Pty. Ltd.
4 Lentara Court
Cheltenham, Victoria, 3192 Australia
Email: info@halleonard.com.au

MIYA SAMA
from THE MIKADO

Words by W.S. Gilbert
Music by Arthur Sullivan

THE WAYFARING STRANGER

American Folksong
Arranged by Bill Boyd

LOVE SONG
(Caro mio ben)

Giuseppe Giordani

CHINATOWN, MY CHINATOWN

Words by William Jerome
Music by Jean Schwartz
Arranged by Bill Boyd

THE ERIE CANAL

American Folksong
Arranged by Bill Boyd

LOCH LOMOND

Scottish Folksong
Arranged by Bill Boyd

MIYA SAMA
from THE MIKADO

TUBA

Words by W.S. Gilbert
Music by Arthur Sullivan

THE WAYFARING STRANGER

American Folksong
Arranged by Bill Boyd

TUBA

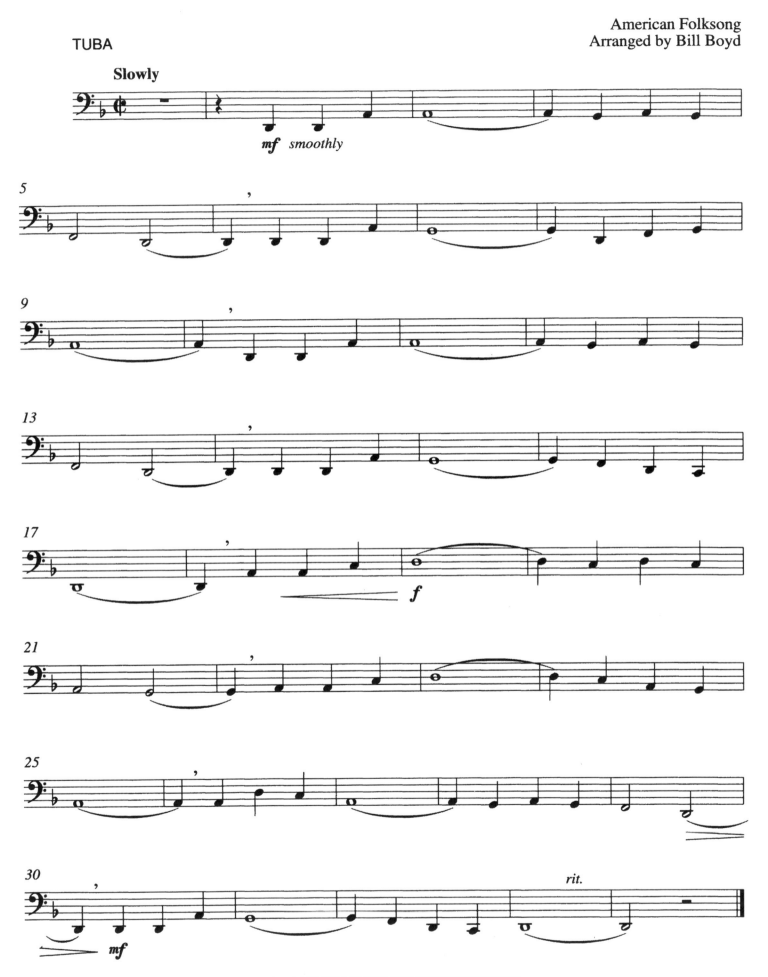

LOVE SONG
(Caro mio ben)

TUBA

Giuseppe Giordani

CHINATOWN, MY CHINATOWN

Words by William Jerome
Music by Jean Schwartz
Arranged by Bill Boyd

TUBA

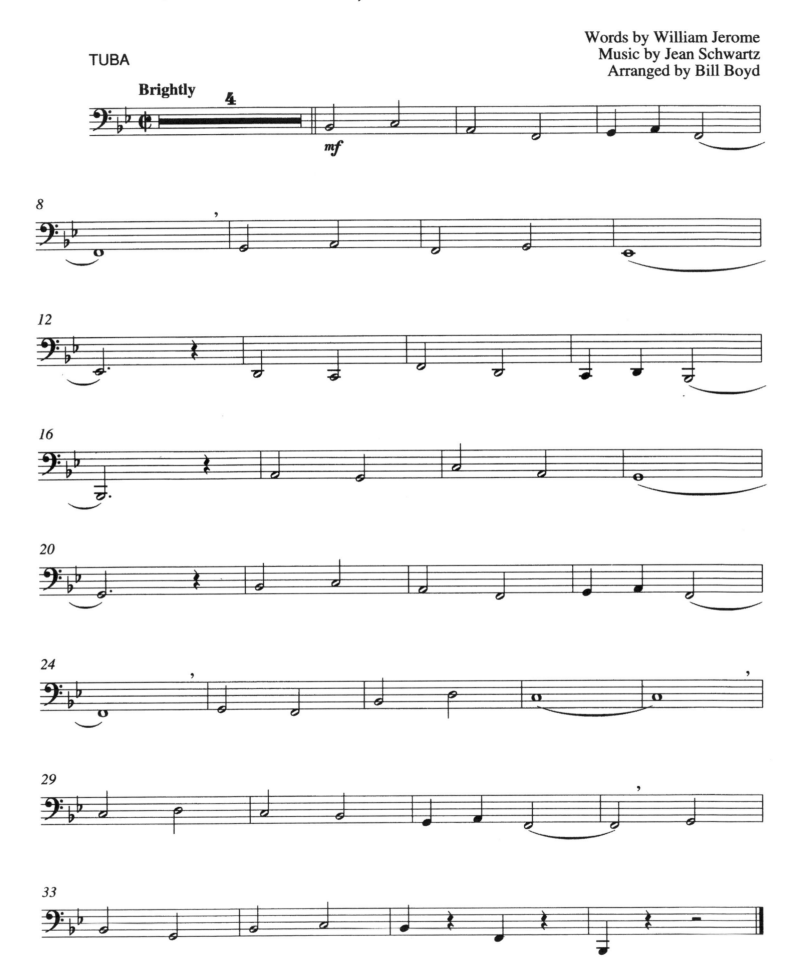

THE ERIE CANAL

TUBA

American Folksong
Arranged by Bill Boyd

LOCH LOMOND

Scottish Folksong
Arranged by Bill Boyd

TUBA

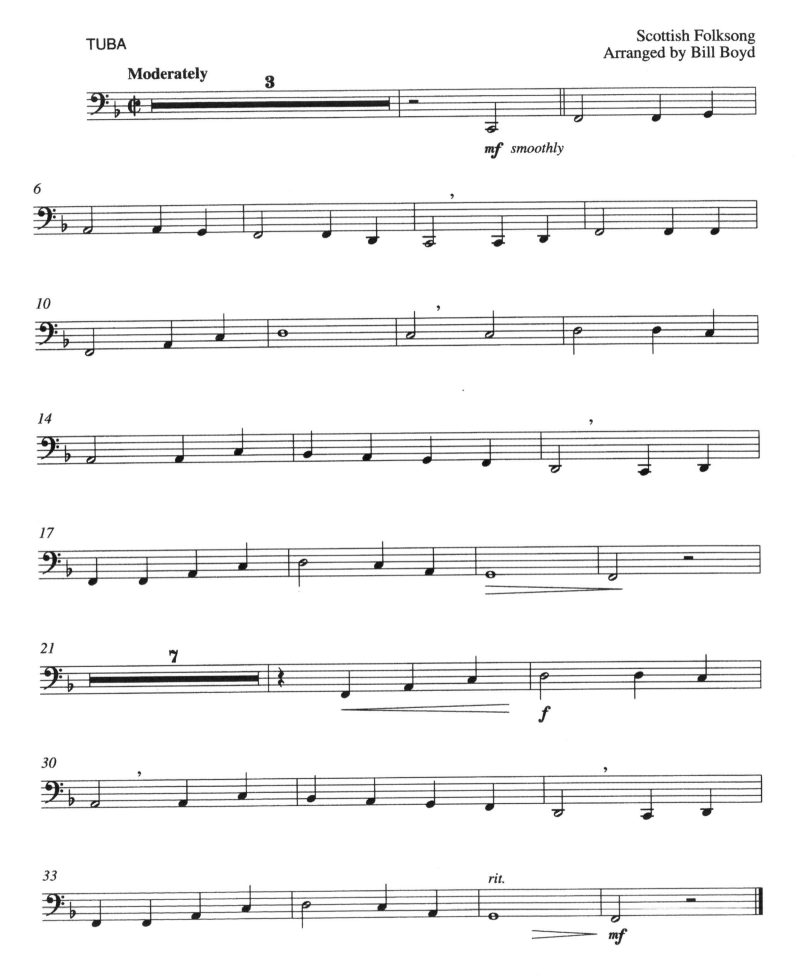

COME, THOU FOUNT OF EVERY BLESSING

TUBA

American Folk Hymn
Arranged by Bill Boyd

8

LENTO

ll

George Frideric Handel

TUBA

opyright © 1992 HAL LEONARD PUBLISHING CORPORATION
International Copyright Secured   All Rights Reserved

THE LAST SATURDAY EVENING

TUBA

Edvard Grieg

opyright © 1992 HAL LEONARD PUBLISHING CORPORATION
International Copyright Secured   All Rights Reserved

REPENTANCE
(Chi sprezzando)
from THE PASSION

TUBA

George Frideric Handel

THE LONELY FOREST
(Bois Épais)

TUBA

Jean-Baptiste Lully

HEY, HO! NOBODY HOME

TUBA

English Folksong
Arranged by Bill Boyd

COME, THOU FOUNT OF EVERY BLESSING

American Folk Hymn
Arranged by Bill Boyd

LENTO

George Frideric Handel

THE LAST SATURDAY EVENING

Edvard Grieg

REPENTANCE

(Chi sprezzando)
from THE PASSION

George Frideric Handel

THE LONELY FOREST
(Bois Épais)

Jean-Baptiste Lully

HEY, HO! NOBODY HOME

English Folksong
Arranged by Bill Boyd